# THE STORY OF
# AMERICA
## THE FIRST 500 YEARS

The Story of America is one of movement—
From its discovery and early exploration,
To the establishment of one nation—
From its colonization by European powers,
To the great immigrations and Westward expansion—
From the age of scientific discoveries and invention,
To voyages beyond the bonds of earth and into space—
The Story of America continues.

# from THE COMING AMERICAN

Sam W. Foss

Bring me men to match my mountains,
  Bring me men to match my plains;
Men with empires in their purpose,
  And new eras in their brains.
Bring me men to match my prairies,
  Men to match my inland seas;
Men whose thoughts shall prove a highway
  Up to ample destinies;
Bring me men to match my mountains—
  Bring me men.

*Bring me men to match my forests,*
  *Strong to fight the storm and blast,*
*Branching toward the skyey future*
  *Rooted in the fertile past;*
*Bring me men to match my valleys,*
  *Tolerant of sun and snow,*
*Men out of whose faithful purpose*
  *Time's consummate blooms shall grow;*
*Men to tame the tigerish instincts*
  *Of the lair, the cave, and den,*
*Cleanse the dragon, slime of nature—*
  *Bring me men.*

Bring me men to match my rivers,
  Continent cleavers, flowing free;
Men of oceanic impulse,
  Men whose moral currents sweep
Toward the wide-infolding ocean
  Of the undiscovered deep;
Men who feel the strong pulsation
  Of the central sea, and then
Time their current to its throb—
  Bring me men.

Many scholars believe that approximately 500 years before Columbus Norse mariner and adventurer Leif Ericson was the first European to reach the New World. Ericson named his discovery Vinland because of the great number of grapevines he found. Vinland has been variously identified as the coast of Labrador, Newfoundland, or New England. This painting by an unknown artist depicts the first sighting of land by Ericson.

# THE VOICE THAT BEAUTIFIES THE LAND

Navajo

The voice that beautifies the land!
The voice above,
The voice of the thunder,
Among the dark clouds
Again and again it sounds,
The voice that beautifies the land.

The voice that beautifies the land!
The voice below,
The voice of the grasshopper,
Among the flowers and grasses
Again and again it sounds,
The voice that beautifies the land.

Archaeologists believe the elaborate cliff dwellings at the Navajo National Monument in northeastern Arizona were built in the early part of the thirteenth century by the Anasazi culture. The Betatakin Cliff Dwelling, pictured here, is the most accessible of the many dwellings. This structure contains 135 rooms, but the largest of the many cliff dwellings contains over 300 rooms. By 1300, drought and erosion had caused the Anasazi to abandon these homes; they lay vacant until the Navajos settled here in the nineteenth century.

As school children know, in 1492, Columbus "sailed the ocean blue" in the *Niña*, the *Pinta*, and the *Santa María*. An experienced navigator, Columbus hoped to discover a route to the East Indies by sailing west across the Atlantic. Although he never sighted the North American mainland, he explored several Caribbean islands, including Jamaica and Cuba. Upon his return to Spain, Columbus was made governor of those lands. He made three more trips to the New World before his death in 1506. This painting by an unknown artist depicts his first voyage.

6

# from COLUMBUS

Joaquin Miller

Behind him lay the gray Azores,
  Behind the Gates of Hercules;
Before him not the ghost of shores,
  Before him only shoreless seas.
The good mate said: "Now must we pray,
  For lo! the very stars are gone.
Brave Admiral, speak, what shall I say?"
  "Why, say 'Sail on! sail on! and on'!"

"My men grow mutinous day by day;
  My men grow ghastly wan, and weak."
The stout mate thought of home; a spray
  Of salt wave washed his swarthy cheek.
"What shall I say, brave Admiral, say,
  If we sight naught but seas at dawn?"
"Why, you shall say at break of day,
  'Sail on! sail on! sail on! and on'!"

They sailed. They sailed.
  Then spake the mate:
  "This mad sea shows his teeth to-night.
He lifts his lip, he lies in wait,
  With lifted teeth, as if to bite!
Brave Admiral, say but one good word:
  What shall we do when hope is gone?"
The words leapt like a leaping sword:
  "Sail on! sail on! sail on! and on!"

Then, pale and worn, he kept his deck,
  And peered through darkness.
  Ah, that night
Of all dark nights! And then a speck—
  A light! a light! a light! a light!
It grew, a starlit flag unfurled!
  It grew to be Time's burst of dawn.
He gained a world; he gave that world
  Its grandest lesson: "On! sail on!"

# PONCE DE LEON

Edith M. Thomas

You that crossed the ocean old,
Not from greed of Inca's gold,
But to search by vale and mount,
Wood and rock, the wizard fount
Where Time's harm is well undone,—
Here's to Ponce de Leon.
And your liegemen every one!

Surely, still beneath the sun,
In some region further west,
You live in and have your rest,
While the world goes spinning round,
And the sky hears the resound
Of a thousand shrill new fames,
Which your jovial silence shames!

Strength and joys your days endow,
Youth's eyes glow beneath your brow;
Wars and vigils are forgot,
And the Scytheman threats you not.
Tell us, of your knightly grace,
Tell us, left you not some trace
Leading to that well spring true
Where old souls their age renew?

The building pictured dates from 1700 and is one of the oldest in
Saint Augustine, Florida, which is recognized as the oldest, contin-
ually occupied city in the United States. Founded in 1565, Saint
Augustine was the northernmost outpost of Spain's New World empire.
Just fifty years earlier, Spanish adventurer, Ponce de Leon, explored the
coast of Florida, which he thought was an island. Saint Augustine was con-
trolled by Spain until it was taken by the British in 1763. In 1821, the city
and its fortress passed into American hands.

# from WRITINGS

Fray Junípero Serra

The day came. A little chapel and altar were erected
in that little valley, and under the same live-oak
close to the beach where, it is said, Mass was cele-
brated at the beginning of the last century.
Two processions from different directions converged
at the same time on the spot,
one from the sea, and one from the land expedition;
we singing the divine praises in the launch,
and the men on land in their hearts.
Our arrival was greeted by the joyful sound
of the bells suspended from the branches
of the oak tree. Everything being in readiness . . .
I intoned the hymn *Veni, Creator Spiritus,*
at the conclusion of which,
and after invoking the help of the Holy Spirit
on everything we were about to perform,
I blessed the salt and the water.
Then we all made our way to a gigantic cross
which was all in readiness and lying on the ground.
With everyone lending a hand
we set it in an upright position. . . .
All the time the bells were ringing,
and our rifles were being fired,
and from the boat came the thunder of big guns.

The *Basilica of Mission San Carlos Borromeo del Rio Carmel* in Carmel, California was established by Padre Junípero Serra, a Spanish priest and teacher sent to colonize California in 1769. Concerned with converting the natives to Christianity, Serra founded nine missions along the California coast. Padre Serra died in 1784 and is buried at the Carmel Mission.

# from THE MAYFLOWER

Erastus Wolcott Ellsworth

Down in the bleak December bay
The ghostly vessel stands away;
Her spars and halyards white with ice,
Under the dark December skies.
A hundred souls, in company,
Have left the vessel pensively,—
Have reached the frosty desert there,
And touched it with the knees of prayer.
    And now the day begins to dip,
The night begins to lower
      Over the bay, and over the ship
      Mayflower.

Neither the desert nor the sea
Imposes rites: their prayers are free;
Danger and toil the wild imposes,
And thorns must grow before the roses.
And who are these?—and what distress
The savage-acred wilderness
On mother, maid, and child may bring,
Beseems them for a fearful thing;
    For now the day begins to dip,
The night begins to lower
      Over the bay, and over the ship
      Mayflower.

Thinking of England and of home:
Might they—the Pilgrims, there and then
Ordained to do the work of men—
Have seen, in visions of the air,
While pillowed on the breast of prayer

    (When now the day began to dip,
The night began to lower
      Over the bay, and over the ship
      Mayflower),

The Canaan of their wilderness
A boundless empire of success;
And seen the years of future nights
Jewelled with myriad household lights;

And seen the honey fill the hive;
And seen a thousand ships arrive;
And heard the wheels of travel go;
It would have cheered a thought of woe.

    When now the day began to dip,
The night began to lower
      Over the bay, and over the ship
      Mayflower.

The *Mayflower II*, seen under sail in a painting by American artist Marshall Joyce, was built in 1955 as a joint venture between the English company, Project Mayflower, and Plimoth Plantation. Although the reproduction had to meet modern safety standards, it is an exact replica of the ship that brought 102 Pilgrims to America on a sixty-six-day voyage in 1620. The *Mayflower II* lies moored at Plimoth Plantation in Plymouth, Massachusetts, and is staffed by costumed guides who portray the passengers and crew of the original *Mayflower*.

In 1607, Captain John Smith established the first permanent English settlement in America at Jamestown, Virginia. All that remain above ground are the ruins of the old church tower which was built in 1640. Visitors to Jamestown can see foundations of public buildings and houses, remains of streets, and a variety of artifacts, all recently unearthed through archeological research.

# from A LETTER BY CAPTAIN JOHN SMITH

. . . We are now remaining
being in good health,
all our men well contented,
free from mutinies,
in love with one another;
and as we hope in continual peace
with the Indians, where we doubt not,
by God's gracious assistance
and the adventurers' willing minds
and speedy furtherance
to so honorable action,
in after times to see our nation
to enjoy a country not only exceeding
pleasant for habitation
but also very profitable
for commerce in general,
no doubt pleasing to almighty God,
honorable to our gracious sovereign,
commodious generally
to the whole Kingdom.

# ON LIBERTY

John Winthrop

Man, as he stands
in relation to man
simply hath liberty
to do what he lists;
it is a liberty to do evil
as well as good.
This liberty is incompatible
and inconsistent with authority.

. . . But if you will be satisfied
to enjoy such civil
and lawful liberties,
such as Christ allows you,
then will you quietly
and cheerfully submit
unto that authority
which is set over you
. . . for your good.

This full-scale replica of Plimoth Plantation is an exact recreation of the colony during the early 1600s and is similar to other New England colonies of that time. Costumed guides demonstrate seventeenth-century crafts at the colony's meetinghouse, houses, gardens, and workshops. Twelve-time governor of the Massachusetts Bay Colony, John Winthrop, was responsible for bringing many English to the New World.

# from CRISIS PAPERS

Thomas Paine

These are the times
that try men's souls.

The summer soldier
and the sunshine patriot will,
in this crisis,
shrink from the service
of their country;

but he that stands it now,
deserves the love and thanks
of man and woman.

English-born writer, Thomas Paine immigrated to America in 1774. Just two years later, he wrote his highly influential pamphlet, *Common Sense*, which urged the colonists to declare independence from England. *The Crisis Papers* were written to inspire the Continental Army. After the Revolution, Paine returned to England and subsequently became involved in the French Revolution. He returned to America in 1802 and died a few years later in obscurity. This painting, attributed to Bass Otis, hangs in the Huntington Museum in San Marino, California.

PAUL•REVERE

# from PAUL REVERE'S RIDE

Henry Wadsworth Longfellow

Listen, my children, and you shall hear
Of the midnight ride of Paul Revere,
On the eighteenth of April, in seventy-five;
Hardly a man is now alive
Who remembers that famous day and year.

He said to his friend, "If the British march
By land or sea from town to-night,
Hang a lantern aloft in the belfry arch
Of the North Church tower as a signal light,—
One, if by land, and two, if by sea;
And I on the opposite shore will be,
Ready to ride and spread the alarm
Through every Middlesex village and farm,
For the country folk to be up and to arm."

Then he said, "Good night!" and with muffled oar
Silently rowed to the Charleston shore....

Meanwhile, his friend, through alley and street,
Wanders and watches with eager ears,
Till in the silence around him he hears
The muster of men at the barrack door,
The sound of arms, and the tramp of feet,
And the measured tread of the grenadiers,
Marching down to their boats on the shore.

Meanwhile, impatient to mount and ride,
Booted and spurred, with a heavy stride
On the opposite shore walked Paul Revere.
And lo! as he looks, on the belfry's height
A glimmer, and then a gleam of light!
He springs to the saddle, the bridle he turns,
But lingers and gazes, till full on his sight
A second lamp in the belfry burns!

It was twelve by the village clock,
When he crossed the bridge into Medford town.
He heard the crowing of the cock,
And the barking of the farmer's dog,
And felt the damp of the river fog,
That rises after the sun goes down.

It was one by the village clock,
When he galloped into Lexington.
He saw the gilded weathercock
Swim in the moonlight as he passed,
And the meeting-house windows, blank and bare,
Gazed at him with a spectral glare.

It was two by the village clock,
When he came to the bridge in Concord town.
He heard the bleating of the flock,
And the twitter of birds among the trees,
And felt the breath of the morning breeze
Blowing over the meadows brown.

So through the night rode Paul Revere;
And so through the night went his cry of alarm
To every Middlesex village and farm,—
A cry of defiance and not of fear,
A voice in the darkness, a knock at the door,
And a word that shall echo forevermore!

For, borne on the night-wind of the Past,
Through all our history, to the last,
In the hour of darkness and peril and need,
The people will waken and listen to hear
The hurrying hoof-beats of that steed,
And the midnight message of Paul Revere.

On April 18, 1775, the silversmith Paul Revere road into history with his midnight ride which alerted the American patriots of the impending arrival of British troops. At dawn the next day, fifty or sixty minutemen met 700 British regulars at Lexington Green. No one knows who fired the first shot, but eight Americans were killed. The British regrouped and marched on to Concord where they met 400 minutemen. In a bloody battle, the British were routed that historic day, and the American War for Independence had begun.

# from A LETTER TO THE CONTINENTAL CONGRESS

John Paul Jones

I trust that I have . . . made fairly clear
to you the tremendous responsibilities
that devolve upon
the Honorable Committee
of which you are a member.
You are called upon to found a new navy;
to lay the foundations
of a new power afloat
that must some time . . .
become formidable enough
to dispute even with England
the mastery of the ocean.
Neither you nor I may live
to see such growth.
But we are here at
the planting of the tree
and maybe some of us must,
in the course of destiny,
water its feeble and struggling roots
with our blood.
If so, let it be so! We cannot help it.
We must do the best we can
with what we have at hand!

The Chapel of the Naval Academy, founded in 1845 in Annapolis, Maryland, features beautiful stained-glass windows designed by Charles Tiffany in honor of John Paul Jones and other Naval heroes. After the end of the American Revolution, Jones served in the Russian navy and died in Paris in 1792. His body was later moved to Annapolis where he is entombed in the Naval Academy Chapel and accorded a twenty-four hour Marine guard.

On the night of December 25, 1776, through a heavy and driving
sleet, General George Washington and his troops crossed the
Delaware River to surprise General Howe and his British forces
camped just north of Trenton, New Jersey. Washington's victory at
Trenton, with an ill-equipped army and against incredible odds, was an
important victory for the American troops. This famous painting, by the
artist Emmanuel Gottlieb Leutze, dates from the mid-1800s and hangs in
the Metropolitan Museum of Art in New York.

# ACROSS THE DELAWARE

Will Carleton

The winter night is cold and drear,
  Along the river's sullen flow;
The cruel frost is camping here—
  The air has living blades of snow.
Look! pushing from the icy strand,
  With ensigns freezing in the air,
There sails a small but mighty band,
  Across the dang'rous Delaware.

Oh, wherefore, soldiers, would you fight
  The bayonets of a winter storm?
In truth it were a better night
  For blazing fire and blankets warm!
We seek to trap a foreign foe,
  Who fill themselves with stolen fare;
We carry freedom as we go
  Across the storm-swept Delaware!

The night is full of lusty cheer
  Within the Hessians' merry camp;
And faint and fainter on the ear
  Doth fall the heedless sentry's tramp.
O hirelings, this new nation's rage
  Is something 'tis not well to dare;
You are not fitted to engage
  These men from o'er the Delaware!

A rush—a shout—a clarion call,
  Salute the early morning's gray:
Now, roused invaders, yield or fall:
  The refuge-land has won the day!
Soon shall the glorious news be hurled
  Wherever men have wrongs to bear;
For freedom's torch illumes the world,
  And God has crossed the Delaware!

# AN INSCRIPTION AT MOUNT VERNON

Washington, the brave, the wise,
the good,
Supreme in war, in council, and
in peace,
Valiant without ambition,
discreet without fear,
Confident without presumption.
In disaster, calm; in success,
moderate; in all, himself.

The hero, the patriot, the Christian.
The father of nations,
the friend of mankind,
Who, when he had won all,
renounced all,
And sought in the bosom of his family
and of nature, retirement,
And in the hope of religion,
immortality.

On the banks of the Potomac River just outside Washington, D.C., stands Mount Vernon, the home of George Washington. The house was originally built by his half-brother, Lawrence, in 1743. Eleven years later, the general and his wife took possession of it, enlarged the main house, added various outbuildings, and landscaped the grounds. It remained Washington's home for the rest of his life, and he is buried on the grounds. The estate is a treasure-house of Washington memorabilia and a valuable source of information about early American life.

# PREAMBLE TO THE CONSTITUTION

We the people
of the United States,
in Order to form
a more perfect Union,
establish Justice,
insure domestic Tranquility,
provide for the common defense,
promote the general Welfare,
and secure the
Blessings of Liberty
to ourselves
and our Posterity,
do ordain and establish
this Constitution for the
United States of America.

Independence Hall in Philadelphia, Pennsylvania, is the site of many momentous occasions in United States' history. Here, in 1775, George Washington accepted the position of Commander-in-Chief of the Continental Army; one year later, the Declaration of Independence was signed; and in 1787, the Constitutional Convention met. The Signing Room, pictured here, appears much as it did in the 1700s.

# from A Defense of the Constitution of Government of the United States of America

John Adams

Let us compare every constitution
we have seen with those
of the United States of America,
and we shall have no reason to blush
for our country.

On the contrary,
we shall feel the strongest motives
to fall upon our knees,
in gratitude to heaven
for having been graciously pleased
to give us birth and education
in that country,
and for having destined us
to live under her laws!

John Adams, our second president, was one of the leaders in America's struggle for independence. During the war, he served abroad as a diplomat, helped to secure French support for America, and later helped negotiate the treaty with England. Second to Washington in the first two presidential elections, he became the nation's first vice-president and was elected as our second president when Washington left office in 1796. This painting, by John Trumble, dates from 1799 and is from the collection of the White House Historical Association.

# MY CREED

Benjamin Franklin

Here is my creed.
I believe in one God,
the creator of the Universe.
That He governs it
by His Providence.

That He ought to be worshiped.
That the most acceptable service
we render to Him
is doing good
to His other children.

That the soul of man is immortal,
and will be treated
with justice in another life
respecting its conduct
in this.

Benjamin Franklin rose from a poor childhood to great wealth by age forty-two to devote himself to public service. Franklin invented bifocals and developed theories on meteorology and ocean currents. In Philadelphia, he helped found an insurance company, hospital, library, and the first militia. A leading proponent of independence, he helped draft the Declaration of Independence and, at age eighty-one, helped form the Constitution. This portrait, by David Martin, is from the collection of the White House Historical Association.

# A NATIONAL PRAYER

Thomas Jefferson

Almighty God, Who has given us this good land
for our heritage, we humbly beseech Thee
that we may always prove ourselves a people mindful
of Thy favor and glad to do Thy will.
Bless our land with honorable industry,
sound learning, and pure manners.

Save us from violence, discord and confusion,
from pride and arrogance,
and from every evil way.
Defend our liberties,
and fashion into one united people
the multitude brought hither
out of many kindreds and tongues.

Endow with the spirit of wisdom those to whom
in Thy Name we entrust
the authority of government,
that there may be justice and peace at home,
and that through obedience to Thy law,
we may show forth Thy praise
among the nations of the earth.

In times of prosperity, fill our hearts
with thankfulness,
and, in the day of trouble,
suffer not our trust in Thee to fail;
all of which we ask through Jesus Christ our Lord.

Amen.

Monticello, Thomas Jefferson's magnificent home on a 640-acre estate near Charlotte, Virginia, was begun in 1770. Jefferson, a scholar, writer, statesman, and architect, planned the neo-classical mansion and moved in even before it was completed. He lived there for fifty-six years until his death; his tomb is nearby. In 1926, the home became a national shrine; it is open to the public.

# THE SPIRIT OF LIBERTY

Alexis de Tocqueville

Local assemblies of the people
constitute the strength
of free nations—
Municipal institutions are to liberty,
what primary schools
are to science:
they bring it within
the people's reach,
and teach them
how to use and enjoy it.

A nation may establish
a system of free government,
but without the spirit
of municipal institutions,
it cannot have
the spirit of liberty.

The Liberty Bell, originally housed in Independence Hall in Philadelphia, was moved in 1976 to a pavilion on Independence Mall. The bell was cast in London and arrived in Philadelphia in 1752; because of a flaw, it was melted down and recast. It rang on many occasions, including the signing of the Declaration of Independence in 1776. There are many stories about the famous crack; during years of the bell's use, many small cracks developed, and no one knows when the fatal crack first appeared.

# WASHINGTON'S MONUMENT

Anonymous

For him who sought his country's good
In plains of war, mid scenes of blood;
Who, in the dubious battle's fray,
Spent the warm noon of life's bright day,
That to a world he might secure
Rights that forever shall endure,
 Rear the monument of fame!
 Deathless is the hero's name!

For him, who when the war was done,
And victory sure, and freedom won,
Left glory's theatre, the field,
The olive branch of peace to wield;
And proved, when at the helm of state,
Though great in war, in peace as great;
 Rear the monument of fame!
 Deathless is the hero's name!

For him, whose worth, though unexpress'd,
Lives cherish'd in each freeman's breast,
Whose name, to patriot souls so dear,
Time's latest children shall revere,
Whose brave achievements praised shall be,
While beats one breast for liberty;
 Rear the monument of fame!
 Deathless is the hero's name!

But why for him vain marbles raise?
Can the cold sculpture speak his praise?
Illustrious shade! we can proclaim
Our gratitude, but not thy fame,
Long as Columbia shall be free,
She lives a monument of thee;
 And may she ever rise in fame,
 To honor thy immortal name!

The Washington Monument, a spectacular 555-foot, white obelisk honoring George Washington, was begun in 1848. Construction stopped in 1854, and the monument stood unfinished at 150 feet for the next twenty years. In 1876, Congress appropriated money to finish the monument, and it was finally capped in 1884. Marble used to face the monument weathered differently over the years; the color break marks the twenty-year pause in the monument's construction.

# I BELIEVE

Theodore Roosevelt

I believe in honesty, sincerity,
    and the square deal;
    in making up one's mind what to
    do—and doing it.

I believe in fearing God
    and taking one's own part.

I believe in hitting the line hard
    when you are right.

I believe in speaking softly
    and carrying a big stick.

I believe in hard work
    and honest sport.

I believe in a sane mind
    in a sane body.

I believe we have room for but one
    sole loyalty, and that is loyalty
    to the American people.

Theodore Roosevelt, our twenty-sixth president, was the twenty-fifth chief executive to live in the White House, which was built during the term of our second president, John Adams. The mansion was heavily damaged during the War of 1812 but was rebuilt, extended, and painted white in 1818. The semicircular south portico, seen here, was added in 1824. Over the years there have been many additions and renovations, including extensive work by First Lady Jacqueline Kennedy in the early 1960s to restore many of the rooms to their original state.

# from THE NAME OF OLD GLORY

James Whitcomb Riley

Old Glory; say, who,
By the ships and the crew,
And the long blended ranks of the gray and the blue—
Who gave you, Old Glory, the name that you bear
With such pride everywhere
As you cast yourself free to the rapturous air
And leap out full length, as we're wanting you to?—
Who gave you that name, with the ring of the same,
And the honor and fame so becoming to you?—
Your stripes stroked in ripples of white and of red,
With your stars at the glittering best overhead—
Who gave you the name of Old Glory?—say, who—
    Who gave you the name of Old Glory?

And it spake, with a shake of the voice, and it said:—
"By the driven snow white and the living blood red
Of my bars, and their heaven of stars overhead—
By the symbol conjoined of them all, skyward cast,
As I float from the steeple, or flap at the mast,
Or droop o'er the sod where the long grasses nod—
My name is as old as the Glory of God.
    So I came by the name of Old Glory."

The legend of Betsy Ross was begun in 1870 by her grandson who told of a committee, headed by George Washington, which asked Ross to stitch a flag for the new country. Despite attempts to verify the story, there is no proof that Betsy Ross actually made the first flag, although she had made flags for ships and for the state of Pennsylvania. In 1898, the Betsy Ross Memorial Association designated her Philadelphia house as the birthplace of the American flag.

# OLD IRONSIDES

Oliver Wendell Holmes

Ay, tear her tattered ensign down!
 Long has it waved on high,
And many an eye has danced to see
 That banner in the sky;
Beneath it rung the battle shout,
 And burst the cannon's roar;—
The meteor of the ocean air
 Shall sweep the clouds no more.

Her deck, once red with heroes' blood,
 Where knelt the vanquished foe,
When winds were hurrying o'er the flood
 And waves were white below,
No more shall feel the victor's tread,
 Or know the conquered knee;—
The harpies of the shore shall pluck
 The eagle of the sea!

Oh better that her shattered hulk
 Should sink beneath the wave;
Her thunders shook the mighty deep,
 And there should be her grave;
Nail to the mast her holy flag,
 Set every threadbare sail,
And give her to the god of storms,
 The lightning and the gale!

The *USS Constitution*, launched in 1797, earned the name "Old Ironsides" because of thick, copper plating on its hull. With its forty-four guns, the *Constitution* won fame during the War of 1812, but by 1828 it was scheduled for demolition. Oliver Wendell Holmes wrote this inspiring poem to gain public support leading to the renovation of the ship and its preservation as a historic site. The *USS Constitution* is docked at the Boston Naval Shipyard.

# from I AM THE FLAG

Lawrence M. Jones

I am a composite being of all the people of America.
I am the union if you are united.
I am one and indivisible if you are undivided.
I am as strong as the weakest link.
I am an emblem of your country.
I am a symbol of the shadow of the real.
I am a sign pointing to past achievements.
I am a promise of greater things for the future.
I am what you make me.
I am purity if you are pure.
I am bravery if you are brave.
I am loyalty if you are loyal.

I am honor if you are honorable.
I am goodness if you are good.
I am hope if you are hopeful.
I am truth if you are true.

I am the Constitution.
I am law and order.
I am tolerance or intolerance as you force me to be.
I am liberty as you understand liberty.
I am as a pillar of fire by night,
but you must provide the fuel.

I march at the head of the column,
but you must carry me on.

I stand for greater and more glorious
achievement  than can be found in recorded
history, but you must be my inspiration.

I AM THE FLAG.

In 1814, after burning Washington, D.C., the British planned an attack on Baltimore. Fort McHenry, in the harbor, withstood a twenty-five-hour bombardment. That night, a young lawyer, Francis Scott Key, watched the battle from an American ship in the river. At dawn, Key could see that the enormous thirty- by forty-two-foot American flag was still waving. This sight so inspired Key that he wrote the words to our national anthem. Today this flag is displayed in the National Museum of American History at the Smithsonian in Washington, D.C.

# from THE NEW IMMIGRANT

Carl Schurz

"Here in America," I wrote to my friend,
"you can see daily how little
a people needs to be governed.
There are governments, but no masters;
there are governors,
but they are only commissioners, agents.

What there is here
of great institutions of learning,
of churches, of great commercial institutions,
lines of communication, etc.,
almost always owes its existence,
not to official authority,
but to the spontaneous co-operation
of private citizens.
Here you witness the productiveness of freedom.
You see a magnificent church—
a voluntary association . . . has founded it;
an orphan asylum built of marble—
a wealthy citizen has erected it;
a university—some rich men have left
a large bequest for educational purposes,
which serves as a capital stock,
and the university then lives, so to speak,
almost on subscriptions; and so on without end.
We learn here how superfluous is the action
not of governments
concerning a multitude of things
in which in Europe it is deemed
absolutely indispensable,
and how the freedom to do something
awakens the desire to do it."

For more than twenty million immigrants, Ellis Island was the last stop on the journey to America and a new life. When Ellis Island first opened as a port of entry in 1892, most immigrants were from England, Ireland, and the British Isles. By the early years of the twentieth century, the majority of immigrants were coming to America from Eastern European countries. Wherever the people came from, however, they came with one goal in mind—to become free Americans.

# from WHAT IS AN AMERICAN?

Michel Guillaume Jean de Crevecoeur

What then is the American, this new man? He is either an European or the descendant of an European, hence that strange mixture of blood, which you will find in no other country. I could point out to you a family whose grandfather was an Englishman, whose wife was Dutch, whose son married a French woman, and whose present four sons have now four wives of different nations. *He* is an American who, leaving behind him all his ancient prejudices and manners, receives new ones from the new mode of life he has embraced, the new government he obeys, and the new rank he holds. He becomes an American by being received in the broad lap of our great *Alma Mater*. Here individuals of all nations are melted into a new race whose labors and posterity will one day cause great changes in the world. Americans are the western pilgrims who are carrying along with them that great mass of arts, sciences, vigor, and industry which began long since in the east; they will finish the great circle.

The Americans were once scattered all over Europe; here they are incorporated into one of the finest systems of population which has ever appeared and which will hereafter become distinct by the power of the different climates they inhabit. The American ought therefore to love this country much better than that wherein either he or his forefathers were born. Here the rewards of his industry follow with equal steps the progress of his labor; his labor is founded on the basis of nature, *self-interest*; can it want a stronger allurement? Wives and children, who before in vain demanded of him a morsel of bread, now, fat and frolicsome, gladly help their father to clear those fields whence exuberant crops are to arise to feed and to clothe them all, without any part being claimed, either by a despotic prince, a rich abbot, or a mighty lord.

Here religion demands but little of him, a small voluntary salary to the minister, and gratitude to God; can he refuse these? The American is a new man, who acts upon new principles; he must therefore entertain new ideas and form new opinions. From involuntary idleness, servile dependence, penury and useless labor, he has passed to toils of a very different nature, rewarded by ample subsistence. This is an American.

The Amana settlers came from Germany seeking religious freedom. They first settled in New York in 1842 and then moved to Iowa in 1855, where they built seven villages on 26,000 acres of woods and farmland. Everything was owned in common, continuing a practice of religious communal living that lasted until 1932, when Amana became a profit-sharing corporation. Today, Amana is maintained as a historical and cultural attraction, and the Amana Society is engaged in a variety of business enterprises.

This painting by famed western artist Charles M. Russell dates from 1905 and depicts the Lewis and Clark expedition on the Lower Columbia River. For eighteen months, beginning in the summer of 1804, Meriwether Lewis, William Clark, their Native American guide Sacajawea, and a band of men explored the Louisiana Purchase for President Thomas Jefferson. Starting in Saint Louis, they traveled the length of the Missouri River, crossed the Rockies, and continued down the river they named Columbia, until they reached the Pacific Ocean.

# from THE LEWIS AND CLARK EXPEDITION

Meriwether Lewis

## Thursday, November 7, 1805

Here the mountainous country again approaches the river on the left, and a higher mountain is distinguished towards the southwest. At a distance of twenty miles from our camp we halted at a village of Wahkiacums . . . situated at the foot of the high hills on the right, behind two small marshy islands. We merely stopped to purchase some food and two beaver skins, and then proceeded. Opposite to these islands the hills on the left retire, and the river widens into a kind of bay crowded with low islands, subject to be overflowed occasionally by the tide. We had not gone far from this village when the fog cleared off, and we enjoyed the delightful prospect of the ocean; that ocean, the object of all our labours, the reward of all our anxieties. This cheering view exhilarated the spirits of all the party, who were still more delighted on hearing the distant roar of the breakers. We went on with great cheerfulness under the high mountainous country which continued along the right bank; the shore was however so bold and rocky, that we could not, until after going fourteen miles from the last village, find any spot fit for an encampment. At that distance, having made during the day thirty-four miles, we spread our mats on the ground, and passed the night. . . .

# from MEMOIRS OF MY LIFE

John Charles Frémont

The Bay . . . is separated from the sea by low mountain ranges. Looking from the peaks of the Sierra Nevada, the coast mountains present an apparently continuous line, with only a single gap. . . . This is the entrance to the great bay, and is the only water communication from the coast to the interior country. On the south, the bordering mountains come down in a narrow ridge of broken hills . . . against which the sea breaks heavily. On the northern side, the mountain presents a bold promontory, rising in a few miles to a height of two or three thousand feet. Between these points is the strait—about one mile broad in the narrowest part, and five miles long from the sea to the bay. To the Gate I gave the name of *Chrysopylae*, or Golden Gate; for the same reasons that the harbor of Byzantium (Constantinople afterwards), was called *Chrysoceras*, or Golden Horn.

Directly fronting the entrance, mountains a few miles from the shore rise about two thousand feet above the water, crowned by a forest of lofty cypress. . . . Behind, the rugged peak of Mount Diavolo, nearly four thousand feet high, overlooks the surrounding country. . . . It presents a varied character of rugged and broken hills, rolling and undulating land, and rich alluvial shores back by fertile and wooded ranges, suitable for towns, villages, and farms, with which it is beginning to be dotted.

This view of San Francisco Bay with the Golden Gate Bridge illustrates the beauty of the area once described by explorer John Charles Frémont. In the 1840s, Frémont led a number of expeditions throughout the West to mark trails and passes through the Rocky Mountains. He was most fond of the San Francisco Bay area, and the vivid descriptions in his books and government reports led many people to settle near the Bay.

# GO WEST!

Horace Greeley

If any young man is about
to commence in the world,
with little in his circumstances
to prepossess him in favor
of one section above another,
we say to him
publically and privately,
Go to the West;
there your capacities
are sure to be appreciated
and your industry and energy
rewarded.

Almost as quickly as passes and trails were mapped, settlers moved west. Imposing rivers and mountains did little to slow the westward expansion. At least 10,000 pioneers made the arduous trip along the Oregon Trail during the 1840s. The trail began in Kansas, followed the North Platte River through Nebraska to Wyoming, and continued along the Snake River to the Oregon Territory. The trail along the Snake River and through the Grand Teton Range of the Rocky Mountains, pictured here, was one of the most difficult crossings of the 2,000 mile trek.

57

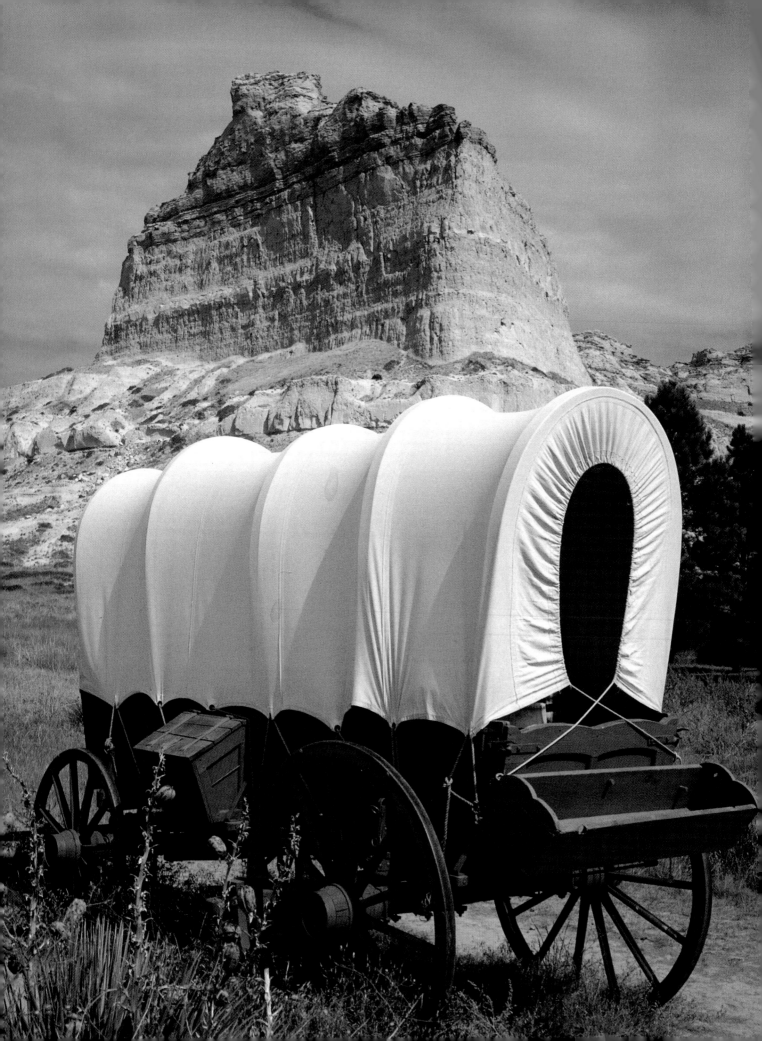

# from PIONEERS! O PIONEERS!

Walt Whitman

O you youths, Western youths,
So impatient, full of action, full of manly pride and friendship,
Plain I see you Western youths, see you tramping with the foremost,
    Pioneers! O Pioneers!

Have the elder races halted?
Do they drop and end their lesson, wearied over there beyond the sea?
We take up the task eternal, and the burden and the lesson,
    Pioneers! O Pioneers!

All the past we leave behind,
We debouch upon a newer mightier world, varied world,
Fresh and strong the world we seize, world of labor and the march,
    Pioneers! O Pioneers!

Colorado men are we,
From the peaks gigantic, from the great sierras and the high plateaus,
From the mine and from the gully, from the hunting trail we come,
    Pioneers! O Pioneers!

From Nebraska, from Arkansas,
Central inland race are we, from Missouri,
  with continental blood intervein'd,
All the hands of comrades clasping, all the Southern, all the Northern,
    Pioneers! O Pioneers!

Scott's Bluff, which rises 800 feet above the surrounding North Platte River valley, was an important landmark on the Oregon Trail. Named for a trapper who died in the area in the 1820s, the monument and museum on this site mark successive periods in the settlement of the West. Remains of the famous trail, ruts worn deep by wagon wheels, are still visible.

# from STEAMBOATS ON THE MISSISSIPPI

Mark Twain

And the boat is rather a handsome sight, too. She is long and sharp and trim and pretty, she has two tall, fancy-topped chimneys, with a gilded device of some kind swung between them; a fanciful pilothouse, all glass and "gingerbread," perched on top of the texas deck behind them; the paddleboxes are gorgeous with a picture or with gilded rays above the boat's name; the boiler deck, the hurricane deck, the texas deck are fenced and ornamented with clean white railings; there is a flag gallantly flying from the jackstaff; the furnace doors are open and the fires glaring bravely; the upper decks are black with passengers; the captain stands by the big bell, calm, imposing, the envy of all; great volumes of the blackest smoke are rolling and tumbling out of the chimneys—a husbanded grandeur created with a bit of pitch pine just before arriving at a town; the crew are grouped on the forecastle; the broad stage is run far out over the port bow, and an envied deckhand stands picturesquely on the end of it with a coil of rope in his hand; the pent steam is screaming through the gaugecocks; the captain lifts his hand, a bell rings, the wheels stop; then they turn back, churning the water to foam, and the steamer is at rest.

QUEEN OF THE WEST

R ounding a Bend," credited to F. Palmer, is from a lithograph by Currier and Ives. Utilizing the talents of many different artists, Currier and Ives produced popular prints covering almost all aspects of life during the mid 1800s. The Mississippi River was a popular subject; writer Samuel Langhorne Clemens took the pen name Mark Twain (a riverboat term) after his career as a pilot aboard Mississippi River steamboats. His love of the river is apparent in many of his books, including *Life on the Mississippi* and *The Adventures of Tom Sawyer*.

# FIFTEEN YEARS ON THE ERIE CANAL

Thomas S. Allen

I've got an old mule and her name is Sal,
Fifteen years on the Erie Canal.
She's a good old worker and a good old pal,
Fifteen years on the Erie Canal.
We've hauled some barges in our day,
Filled with lumber, coal, and hay,
And ev'ry inch of the way I know,
From Albany to Buffalo.

Low bridge, ev'rybody down,
Low bridge, we must be getting near a town,
You can always tell your neighbor,
You can always tell your pal,
If he's ever navigated on the Erie Canal.

Massive engineering feats were necessary to construct locks and tunnels, such as the Paw Paw tunnel on the Chesapeake and Ohio Canal, pictured here. Glorified in song and poem, canals such as the Erie, the Union Canal of Pennsylvania, and the Chesapeake and Ohio moved thousands of settlers and tons of freight. Canal work and travel peaked around 1850. By 1880, railways had taken over, and boat travel on canals dwindled.

## from A LETTER BY SAM HOUSTON

. . . If we were to judge of the future
by the past, it might so happen,
were I settled in a state;
that I might render my aid
in some future political struggle
between usurpation,
and rights of the people in wresting power
from the hands of a corrupt Usurper,
and depositing it,
where the spirit of the constitution,
and will of the people
would wish it placed.
These considerations are not
without their influence,
for I must ever love that country
and its institutions,
which gave Liberty and happiness
to my kindred and friends!
And these blessings can only be preserved
by vigilance and virtue!

San Antonio's earliest mission, the Alamo, pictured here, was established in 1718 and was originally known as *Mission San Antonio de Valero*. In 1836, when Texas fought for independence from Mexico, 188 Americans held off a Mexican force of 5,000 men for two weeks. After repeated assaults, the walls of the Alamo were finally scaled, and all the defenders, including James Bowie and Davy Crockett, were killed. "Remember the Alamo" became the rallying cry for Texas' independence.

# from A TRIBUTE TO ABRAHAM LINCOLN

Carl Sandburg

Among the million words in the Lincoln utterance record, he
interprets himself with a more keen precision than someone
else offering to explain him. . . .
Like an ancient psalmist he warned Congress:
"Fellow citizens, we cannot escape history.
We will be remembered in spite of ourselves.
No personal significance or insignificance can spare
one or another of us. The fiery trial through which we pass
will light us down in honor or dishonor
to the latest generation."
The people of many other countries
take Lincoln now for their own. He belongs to them.
He stands for decency, honest dealing,
plain talk, and funny stories. . . .
He had something they would like to see
spread everywhere over the world.
Democracy? We can't find words to say exactly what it is,
but he had it. In his blood and bones he carried it.
In the breath of his speeches and writing it is there.
Popular government? Republican institutions?
Government where the people have the say-so,
one way or another telling their elected leaders
what they want? He had the idea. It's there in the light
and shadows of his personality, a mystery that can be lived
but never fully spoken in words.
So perhaps we may say that the well-assured
and most enduring memorial to Lincoln
is invisibly there, today, tomorrow
and for a long time yet to come in the hearts
of lovers of liberty, men and women who understand
that wherever there is freedom there have been those
who fought, toiled and sacrificed for it.

The Lincoln Memorial was proposed by Congress upon Lincoln's
assassination but was not begun until 1911, when President Taft
selected the site. Daniel Chester French was selected to design
what became one of the most famous monuments in America. Stone
carvers worked four years to carve the statue from twenty blocks of Georgia
marble, and the monument was dedicated in 1922. There have been many
tributes to Lincoln over the years; this speech was delivered to Congress by
fellow Illinoisian and poet Carl Sandburg on Lincoln's birthday in 1959.

# from A LETTER BY SULLIVAN BALLOU

My very dear wife,

The indications are very strong that we shall move in a few days perhaps tomorrow. And lest I should not be able to write you again, I feel impelled to write a few lines that may fall under your eye when I am no more. Our movement may be one of a few days duration and full of pleasure. And it may be one of severe conflict and death to me. . . . I know how American civilization now bears upon the triumph of the Government and how great a debt we owe to those who went before us . . . and I am willing, perfectly willing, to lay down all my joys in this life to help maintain this government and to pay that debt.

I cannot describe to you my feelings on this calm summer night when two thousand men are sleeping around me. A pure love of my country and of the principles I have advocated before the people and the name of honor that I love more than I fear death have called upon me and I have obeyed.

I know I have but few claims upon Divine Providence but something whispers to me. Perhaps it is the wafted prayer of my little Edgar that I shall return to my loved one unharmed. If I do not, my dear Sarah, never forget how much I loved you, nor that when my last breath escapes me on the battlefield it will whisper your name.

But Oh Sarah! If the dead can come back to this earth . . . I shall be always with you in the brightest day and the darkest night, amidst your happiest scenes and gloomiest hours, always and always. And when the soft breeze fans your cheek, it shall be my breath or the cool air your throbbing temple, it shall be my spirit passing by. Sarah, do not mourn me dead. Think I am gone and wait for me, for we shall meet again.

One of the worst battles of the Civil War was fought here in Gettysburg, Pennsylvania, in July, 1863. Even though there were over 40,000 Union and Confederate casualties, the battle marked a turning point for the Union in the war. Less than two years later, the Confederate States surrendered, and the Union was preserved. Civil War soldier Sullivan Ballou's dramatic letter, written on July 14, 1861, was the last received by his wife, Sarah, in Illinois; he was killed the following week at the first battle of Bull Run.

Within Arlington National Cemetery are the graves of thousands of American service men and women, as well as many noted Americans, including President Kennedy, Oliver Wendell Holmes, Generals John J. Pershing and George C. Marshall, and Admirals Robert E. Peary and Richard E. Byrd. On the hill overlooking the cemetery is the Custis-Lee Mansion, which belonged to General Robert E. Lee. In 1861, at the onset of the Civil War, the house and grounds were seized by the Union in order to fortify the area surrounding Washington, D. C.

# LONG, TOO LONG, AMERICA

Walt Whitman

Long, too long America,
Traveling roads all even and peaceful you
   learn'd from joys and prosperity only,
But now, ah now, to learn
   from cries of anguish,
   advancing, grappling with direst fate
   and recoiling not,
And now to conceive and show
   to the world what
   your children enmasse really are.

# from WHAT THE ENGINES SAID

Bret Harte

What was it the Engines said,
Pilots touching,—head to head
Facing on the single track,
Half a world behind each back?
This is what the engines said,
Unreported and unread.

With a prefatory screech,
In a florid Western speech,
Said the Engine from the West;
"I am from Sierra's crest;
And if altitude's a test,
Why, I reckon, it's confessed
That I've done my level best."

Said the Engine from the East:
"They who work best talk the least,
S'pose you whistle down your breaks;
What you've done is no great shakes,—
Pretty fair,—but let our meeting
Be a different kind of greeting.
Let those folks with champagne stuffing,
Not their Engines, do the puffing!

That is what the Engines said,
Unreported and unread;
Spoken slightly through the nose,
With a whistle at the close.

On May 10, 1869, the famed Golden Spike Ceremony took place at Promontory Summit in Utah. There were actually two golden spikes and a silver spike, and no one attempted to drive the ceremonial spikes. Instead, holes were drilled in the tie to accommodate the spikes which were removed immediately after the ceremony. The silver spike and one golden spike are in the Stanford University Museum; the other golden spike was lost during the San Francisco earthquake.

Americans have been fascinated with flight since the first, twelve-second flight of the Wright Brothers in 1903 at Kitty Hawk, North Carolina. Planes improved rapidly; and just twenty-four years later, aviator Charles Lindbergh became the first person to fly solo, non-stop across the Atlantic, landing in Paris on May 20, 1927. His plane, *The Spirit of Saint Louis*, is on display at the National Air and Space Museum at the Smithsonian in Washington, D.C.

74

# from THE WRITINGS OF ORVILLE WRIGHT

. . .the ground under you is at first a perfect blur, but as you rise the objects become clearer. At a height of one hundred feet you feel hardly any motion at all, except for the wind which strikes your face.

The operator moves a lever: the right wing rises, the machine swings about to the left. You make a very short turn, yet you do not feel the sensation of being thrown from your seat, so often experienced in automobile and railway travel. The objects on the ground now seem to be moving at much higher speed, though you perceive no change in the pressure of the wind on your face. You know then that you are traveling with the wind.

When you near the starting point, the operator stops the motor while still high in the air. The machine coasts down at an oblique angle to the ground, and after sliding fifty or a hundred feet comes to rest. The motor close beside you kept up an almost deafening roar during the whole flight, yet in your excitement you did not notice it until it stopped!

## from A SPEECH TO CONGRESS

John Fitzgerald Kennedy

Now is the time to take longer strides—
time for a great new enterprise—
time for this nation to take
a clearly leading role in space achievements
which, in many ways,
may hold the key to our future on earth.
. . . I believe that this nation
should commit itself
to achieving the goal,
before this decade is out,
of landing a man on the moon
and returning him safely to earth.
No single space project in this period
will be more impressive to mankind
or more important for
the long-range exploration of space.
And none will be so difficult to accomplish. . . .
Let it be clear that this is a judgment
which the members of the Congress
must finally make. Let it be clear that I am
asking the Congress and the country
to accept a firm commitment
to a new course of action. . . .
I believe we should go to the moon. . . .

P resident Kennedy's speech to Congress on May 25, 1961, spurred the nation's interest in space. Less than a year after the first, short flight of Alan Shepard in 1961, John Glenn completed three orbits of the earth. Successive flights increased in duration, leading to the Apollo moon-landing program. On July 20, 1969, Neil Armstrong became the first person to set foot on the surface of the moon, giving the world a view of Earth from the moon, as pictured here. After several more successful flights to the moon, Apollo 17 made the last U.S. lunar landing in December, 1972.

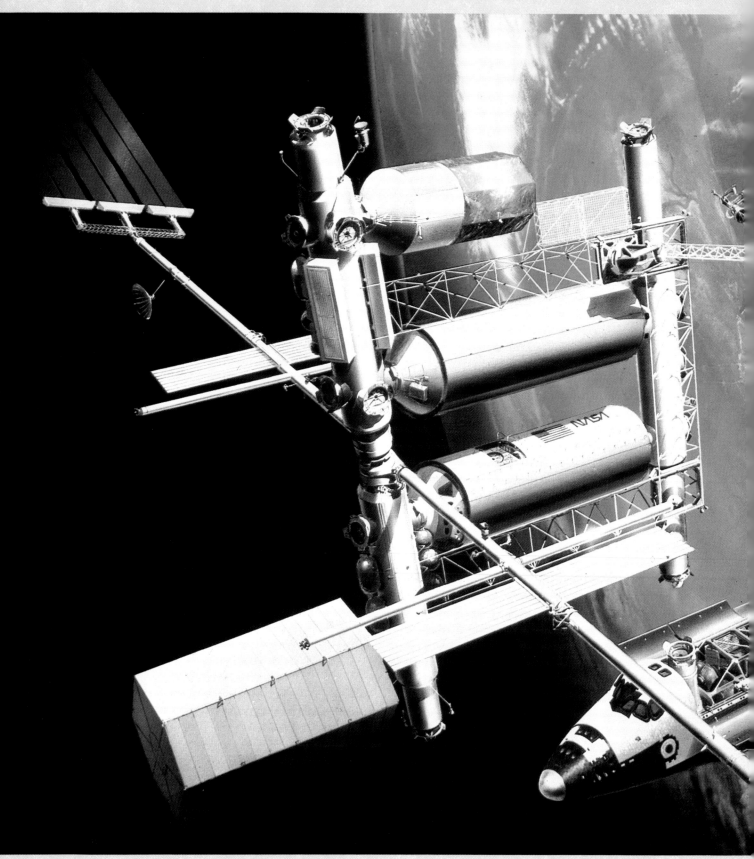

In 1973, scientists began the Skylab missions, and movements toward international cooperation in space were demonstrated by joint missions with the Soviet *Soyuz* space program in 1975. Though progress on an American space station has stalled over the years, plans are still being made to construct a permanent space station such as the one pictured in this NASA painting by artist John J. Olson. The quest for adventure and new frontiers that has driven Americans over the past 500 years continues today as we reach beyond the bounds of Earth.

# HIGH FLIGHT

John Gillespie Magee, Jr.

Oh! I have slipped the surly bonds of Earth
And danced the skies on laughter-silvered wings;
Sunward I've climbed, and
  joined the tumbling mirth
Of sun-split clouds—and done a hundred things
You have not dreamed of—
  wheeled and soared and swung
High in the sunlit silence. Hov'ring there,
I've chased the shouting wind along, and flung
My eager craft through footless halls of air. . . .

Up, up the long, delirious, burning blue
I've topped the wind-swept heights
  with easy grace,
Where never lark, or even eagle, flew;
And, while with silent, lifting mind I've trod
The high untrespassed sanctity of space,
Put out my hand, and touched the face of God.

## PHOTOGRAPHER'S INDEX

2-3, *Leif Ericson*, The Bettmann Archive; 4, Navajo National Monument, Superstock; 6-7, *Niña, Pinta, and Santa Maria*, The Bettmann Archive; 9, Saint Augustine, Florida, Superstock; 10, Basilica of Mission San Carlos Borromeo del Rio Carmel, Superstock; 13, *The Mayflower II*, Photo courtesy of Plimoth Plantation Inc., Plymouth, Massachusetts; 14-15, Jamestown, photo courtesy of National Park Service, Colonial National Historical Park; 16-17, Plimoth Plantation, © Michael Freeman, Photographer; 19, *Thomas Paine*, The Huntington Library and Art Gallery; 20, Paul Revere Statue, Leslie O'Shaughnessy, New England Stock Photography; 22-23, U.S. Naval Academy Chapel, © Michael Freeman, Photographer; 24-25, *Washington Crossing the Delaware*, Superstock; 26-27, Mount Vernon, © 1991, Jake McGuire, Washington Stock Photo, Inc.; 28, Independence Hall, H. Armstrong Roberts; 30, *John Adams*, © by the White House Historical Association, photograph by the National Geographic Society; 33, *Benjamin Franklin*, © by the White House Historical Association, photograph by the National Geographic Society; 35, Monticello, © 1991, Jake McGuire, Washington Stock Photo, Inc.; 36, Liberty Bell, photo courtesy of Philadelphia Convention and Visitors Bureau; 39, Washington Monument, D. Lada, H. Armstrong Roberts; 40-41, The White House, © 1991, Jake McGuire, Washington Stock Photo, Inc.; 42, Betsy Ross House, photo courtesy of Philadelphia Convention and Visitors Bureau; 44-45, USS *Constitution*, Jack Maley, photo courtesy of Massachusetts Office of Travel and Tourism; 46, Stars and Stripes, Smithsonian Institution Photo No. 83-7221; 49, Ellis Island, Superstock; 51, Amana Colonies, B. Vogel, H. Armstrong Roberts; 52-53, C.M. Russell, *Lewis and Clark on the Lower Columbia*, 1905, 1961.195, Amon Carter Museum, Fort Worth; 54-55, San Francisco Bay, Ed Cooper Photography; 57, Grand Teton Mountains, Jeff Gnass Photography; 58, Scott's Bluff National Monument, Superstock; 60-61, *Rounding a Bend*, Currier & Ives; 62, Chesapeake and Ohio Canal, photo courtesy of C & O Canal National Historical Park; 64-65, The Alamo, Superstock; 66, Lincoln Memorial, © 1991, Jake McGuire, Washington Stock Photo, Inc.; 69, Gettysburg Battlefield, photo courtesy of Gettysburg National Military Park; 70-71, Arlington Cemetery, © Michael Freeman, Photographer; 72-73, Golden Spike Reenactment, photo courtesy Golden Spike National Historic Site; 74-75, *The Spirit of St. Louis*, E.R. Degginger, H. Armstrong Roberts; 76-77, Earth from the Moon, FPG International, 78, *Space Station*, H. Armstrong Roberts

## ACKNOWLEDGMENTS

A LETTER BY SULLIVAN BALLOU from the Adin Ballou Papers, Illinois State Historical Library, Springfield, Illinois; A TRIBUTE TO ABRAHAM LINCOLN by Carl Sandburg, permission granted by Maurice C. Greenbaum and Frank M. Parker, Trustees of the Carl Sandburg Family Trust

**Publisher,** Patricia A. Pingry; **Editor,** D. Fran Morley; **Art Director,** Patrick McRae; **Editorial Assistant,** Tim Hamling; **Cover Illustration** by Patrick McRae